Ambiguous Encounters

Story Times 2

Brindley Hallam Dennis

&

Marilyn Messenger

CONTENTS

Acknowledgments   i

1   Rat Run (BHD)   3

2   Pearl (BHD)   8

3   Petra (BHD)   12

4   High Heels & Kisses   18
    (BHD)

5   Perhaps Tomorrow (BHD)   20

6   Perhaps Today (MM)   26

7   Bookmarked (MM)   32

8   If The Oceans Rise (MM)   37

9   Sleeping (MM)   43

10 Water Wings (MM)   47

ACKNOWLEDGMENTS

Rat Run, **Pearl**, & **Petra** have been performed by **Liars League** in New York and Hong Kong.

High Heels & Kisses was Highly Commended

In an Inktears competition, and included in a Showcase anthology.

Bookmarked has been performed by Liars League in New York
If The Oceans Rise was shortlisted in a HISSAC competition in 2014

1 RAT RUN

Her car was already there, pulled into the lay-bye, facing the oncoming traffic. He pulled in in front of it, nosing his headlights to hers, and switched off the engine.

She was indistinct but recognisable despite the reflection of the trees in her windscreen, and for a moment they sat staring at each other across the curved metal of the bonnets, each wondering if the other would get out of their car first. She flashed the headlights, a pale lightning seen obliquely, and he opened his door and slid out of the driver's seat and walked forward to her passenger door. She looked up at him through the glass and gently patted the empty seat beside her. He looked both ways, as if he were about to cross a busy road, and got into the car.

The lay-by was on the edge of town, tucked under a breaking wave of tall and overarching full leafed trees, mirrored on the far side of the road, so that they were in a green tunnel with a narrow band of white sky above, like a strip of torn lace, enclosed by a parted sea of greenery on the bed of which they attempted their escape.

Hello you, she said, looking at him. Her face was soft, relaxed and welcoming. Her smile was faint, comfortable, not threatening. He smiled at her. A car zipped towards them, sped past, and he got the sense of the pale disc of a driver's face turning to face them as it passed. They sat in silence. What was there to say? What was there to say before what was going to be said, in preparation for it?

It's good to see you, he said. She smiled more fully. A vehicle shot from behind them, on the other side of the road, towing a chainsaw of engine noise behind it. A desultory rain of sycamore blossom fell upon the curved bonnets and the slanted windscreens of their cars.

She was twisted in her seat, one heavy breast cupped by the still fastened seat belt. She had one hand on the steering wheel, and the other, the one with which she had patted gently the dark cushion of the passenger seat to invite him in, was now resting on the handbrake. Her legs, lying not quite parallel, firm beneath the dark sheen of her tights, showed below the taught hem of her skirt. Her feet rested in shadow upon the pedals. Out of the corner of his eye he caught sight of another vehicle speeding towards them, its sidelights glittering like bright, inquisitive eyes.

He forced his attention away from the blue car, the same colour as Marge's, and looked into her face. She was still smiling. He should kiss her, he thought, but he should say something first. He could think of nothing to say that was not inane. The weather, work, how the family was, whether or not they had holidays planned.

Are you well?

Yes, and you?

Fine.

Another vehicle sped towards them, rocking her car as it passed, and a lorry, its metal sides rumbling like muffled thunder passed by in the opposite direction. She reached out and took his hand. Her skin was warm, soft, her grip gentle. He did not want more than this, he realised, not right away. This comfortable, not quite comfortable, anticipation, this acceptance, an invitation, a promise. He strove to define his understanding of his feelings.

It's so nice to be here, he said. She leaned forward.

Her lips were so soft. They touched him like a cloud. He closed his eyes. The car shivered again as another zipped by, hooting its horn. He broke away, turned to see a flash of grinning faces and waving hands vanishing from his arc of vision.

I never thought it would so busy, he said.

Never mind that, she said, leaving go of the steering wheel and pulling him onto her by his lapel. It must be a rat-run, he thought, as she kissed him again. The kiss was long, and intense rather than passionate. He wondered where you would rat-run from, where to? Wondered whom he knew who might know of it, who might use it? Who might take such a short-cut? They broke off from the kiss and she sat back in her seat.

What's wrong? She asked, looking at him.

Nothing.

Then kiss me, she said, and he leaned forward and did so, but his mind raced with the cars that raced beside them. They were full of pale turning faces, amazed at the recognition, of his car, parked so strangely there, so obviously. Isn't that Gerry's car? What's he doing this side of town? Isn't that Gerry? Who's that he's with? Perhaps he's broken down, is calling for help. They would ask Marge. Wasn't that Gerry? Didn't I see Gerry? What would he say? To her? To them?

She had taken his hand, was placing it on her leg. That felt nice. But the cars were passing now as if in a race; as if a starting flag had fallen and the narrow avenue beneath the trees were a chicane that they must navigate, jostling for position. She kissed him more urgently, and he felt her loosen the seat belt, and the freed breast flowed against him like a wave. She breathed in deeply as he took it in his palm.

But the cars were streaming now, one after the other, and her car rocked and shook with each one that passed, as if it were being buffeted by gusts of wind, by a storm, by an incoming sea that was closing the gap between the standing waves of trees. The sycamore blossoms were falling thickly, covering the cold glass of the windscreen, darkening the interior of the car where they struggled to connect.

Headlights flashed upon them through the deepening gloom, and the car bucked beneath them, writhing as they kissed, as if it were driven by an ecstatic love. He felt his fingers feeling for her beneath the skirt, the raw tingling smoothness of her tights, the ridge of their seam like an erect clitoris, but the cars still drove, their headlights blazing through the darkness of his consciousness. The rising tide of traffic rattled through like chariots, galloping horses lashed in furious pursuit. He could not hold them back.

She moved away, settled in her seat, her breathing slightly heavy, her face flushed, her eyes bright. He smiled uncertainly, leaning back against the headrest, as if some high water mark had been survived, a tide had turned.

Shall we meet again? she said.

He thought of Marge then, of the sadness. People should not hold themselves back from each other.

Not here, he said.

2 PEARL

Pearl was heavily built and short. People said she cast herself willingly before swine. She was the sort of woman who seemed to invite that titillating speculation about what it would feel like to press various parts of your anatomy against, or even into, various parts of hers.

She had a steady gaze which held you in contempt and seemed to say that if you got the old man out, even if he were standing strictly to attention, she would not be overly impressed. What titillated Jacobson was the thought that she would take it, nevertheless, in her stride, or in her hand, and deal with it efficiently, and without emotion, judging her pleasure, rather than surrendering to it. The thought of being used like that thrilled him to the core.

Rumour in the hotel was that Pearl, who was said to be living out her wild years late in life, following the eventual disintegration of a long standing but too early marriage, would offer relief, of various sorts, to any of the young waiters who were in need.

She can speak with her mouth full in five languages, the handyman said, with a grin.

The handy man kept a tin of heavy duty glue which he sniffed to help him through the day, and at night smoked dope he bought from a man he met at a motorway service station, and drank from bottles of filched spirits he traded with the night porter.

It's possible that Jacobson wouldn't have thought of Pearl in that way, but she had put the idea into his head by telling him that he was too old for her, and that she liked her men vigorous. After that Mae West moment Jacobson became unable to think of her in any other way. He was not comfortable though with the image that the handyman's joke evoked. He did not like to think of Pearl on her knees before anybody, and when he thought of her in relation to himself, he always pictured her as the one standing.

The night of the staff party the hotel was empty and the restaurant closed. If any of the rooms were unexpectedly used before dawn, the housekeeping staff would be perfectly capable of putting them in good order before the next day's guests began to arrive.

Jacobson was standing in the bay window of the lilac sitting room. He looked out through his own reflection towards the front door, where he could see a fat old woman whom he did not at first recognise. It was Pearl. She had lost her aura of confidence. The handyman was leaning close in towards her, his face dark in the orange wash of the porch lights.

Jacobson took a walk to the front door. The handyman, who had already upset several people on the dance floor, was trying to strike a match, but he was holding the box the wrong way round. Pearl, who held an unlit cigarette in slightly trembling fingers, looked towards Jacobson, as if she were really happy to see him.

Let me, Jacobson said, producing the lighter that he always carried in case any of the guests should require a light. He flipped it open, sparked a flame and held it out towards her. She took his hand and drew it closer, and touched the tip of her cigarette to his flame, which flowed towards her as she inhaled. She smiled and stepped back a pace.

Thanks.

The handyman, his mouth hanging open, his face flushed, stood with the matchbox and the unstruck match in his hands. He turned to face Jacobson.

Wha' the fuck are you dooin? He said.

The lady needed a light, Jacobson said, standing motionless beside him.

I was dooin tha', the handyman slurred. Jacobson smiled. The handyman looked at the matchbox, reversed it and struck the match, which flared between them. It was a still night and the flame quickened and burned with a steady glow. After a hot October day, clouds had thickened from the west, keeping the heat in, but not bringing rain.

There was neither moon nor stars, and the three of them stood in the harsh glare of the porch lights, which shone down from the corners of the little pointed roof. The handyman swayed slightly, and the flame shimmied its way along the matchstick until it kissed his finger end.

Fuck! He shook the matchstick to the gravel at his feet. Jacobson could see Pearl, out of the corner of his eye. She was holding the cigarette to her lips between upraised fingers. She seemed shorter than usual.

I need a drink, the handyman said, turning awkwardly and moving unsteadily between them into the warm tunnel of the hallway.

Can I get you a drink? Jacobson asked, when the handyman had gone.

Wine, Pearl said, please.

When he got back, she had finished the cigarette and was leaning against the wooden supports of the porch. Light from the lamps caught the curls of hair at her neck, and shadows slipped down her dress, stroking her calves, and kneeling at her feet.

I brought you white, Jacobson said, holding up the glasses, which he carried, one in each hand. Red for me, he said.

She reached out for the red.

The genuine pearl dissolves in red wine, she said. I thought you'd have known that.

3 PETRA

They say there are two black spots, right in the centre of our circle of vision, that we never see: where the optic nerves join the back of our eyeballs. We overlook them, don't notice them, fill in the detail from what we can see all around.

When Steve told me that he and Jenny had parted I got straight into the car and drove over to see him. I could have phoned; I could have e-mailed; but I wanted to hear it from his own mouth. I wanted him tell me. I wanted to know what had gone wrong.

There was a For Sale sign on a post in the front garden. I said, you're selling the house. He said, yes, that's why there's a For Sale sign in the front garden.

I began to think maybe the e-mail or the phone call would have done as well. I said, where's Jen? He said, she's gone to stay with her mother, until things are sorted out. I wanted to ask what went wrong, but I wanted more for him to tell me without asking. What he didn't tell me was that he was planning to go away. The first I heard of that was about a fortnight later, when Jen called.

Steve's body had been found in Scotland. This is a man, was a man, who lived in the south of England. He had no business in Scotland. He had business up north, unfinished business. Business isn't the right word. It was Petra who lived up north and had done for thirty years.

I knew that they hadn't been in touch for a decade or more, and that before that they hadn't been in touch for a decade or more. A decade before that we had all been great friends. I knew, when I thought about it, that they were due for another episode. Well, I knew that he was.

Petra and I hadn't kept in touch. There was nothing in that. She and I got on fine. It was just that she and I didn't need to keep in touch, not even once a decade. We certainly didn't think about each other all the years in between. When Facebook came in we all connected up again, one by one, except for Steve and Petra. Steve had been thinking of Jen, I supposed.

Steve thought about Petra though. I think he thought about her all the time. He thought about her every day. I saw him regularly. We met up several times a year. Caught up, as they say. He'd ask after Petra, as if he expected me to know.

I haven't heard from her, I'd tell him, not for ages. Petra preyed on his mind. I knew that. She never married. She came close to it once. I'm not sure if she ever knew how close. Well, of course she knew. The time hadn't been right though. Steve missed that boat and caught another one instead, and after that he was playing catch up for the rest of his life.

The last time I saw Steve alive was that time I went over to find out what the hell had gone wrong between him and Jen. Maybe I should have asked her, but I didn't, and besides, what difference would it have made?

There was an inquest. Misadventure was the verdict. Exposure was the cause of death. Jen identified the body. Like a paper doll, she told me. He'd been living rough, they said, but only for a little while. There had been no long, slow deterioration. He had found his way up onto the moors, or whatever they call them up there, had drunk a bottle of whisky, probably in the sun, had taken off all of his clothes, and walked a little further, and lay down, and gone to sleep, and, it being a clear night in May, had frozen to death during the hours of darkness. The S word had been mentioned, but there had been no letter. The balance of his mind had been mentioned. He was going through a divorce, after all. But the S word is a finding that inquests are reluctant to make unless it's absolutely certain.

How did he get there? Jen asked. Why did he go? I wanted the answers to those questions too. That was why I went to see Petra.

I haven't seen him for years, she said. I didn't know he'd moved to Scotland.

He hadn't moved to Scotland, I told her.

What was he doing there? She asked. That wasn't the question, I wanted to tell her. Was he on holiday? She asked.

No, I said. She didn't seem very upset. In fact she didn't seem upset at all.

What are you doing up here anyway? she asked.

I came to see you, I told her. I came to tell you about Steve. I could see the surprise on her face. I think she almost said, why? But she didn't. I could see that she was thinking it though. Why would you come all the way up here to tell me about Steve? He was the love of your life, I wanted to tell her. That's why you never married. You were the love of his life, I said.

Was I?

I didn't believe it. Was she saying that she didn't know? I didn't know what to say. He'd told me so many times, over the years. He'd told me she was the love of his life. He'd told me he was the love of hers. Circumstances, he'd told me, were what had kept them apart.

Love, he used to say, isn't about what you do. It's about how you feel.

We'd get round to it at the end of our conversations, when we

were on the last glass of wine, after the meal. We used to meet up a
couple of times a year, go off somewhere remote; stay in a good hotel.
Have a good meal, share a bottle of wine, a couple of whiskies after. We
wouldn't get drunk, just a little sentimental. Not maudlin exactly,
nostalgic maybe. We'd talk about the past. That's when he'd tell me,
about walking away all those years ago. One little mistake, he used to
say: a turn to the left instead of the right., and you're off the path for
good.

Love, he used to say, is something you only have to recognise.
Once you've done that it never goes away. You only have to know.

You must have known, I said to her.

I haven't seen him for years, she said. I'd only a seen him a couple
of times in the last twenty years.

You hadn't forgotten him though, I said.

No, of course not, she said. We had some good times, she said.
Back when we were all together.

But since then, I wanted to ask her, hadn't you thought about him?
He thought about you all the time, I wanted to tell her. He thought
about you every day.

I often remember those times, she said. Are you still in touch with
Sandra and Jack?

She said no more, and I couldn't bring myself to ask her outright.

Petra's unblinking eyes have haunted me; and her mouth, as if she were about to whisper or to smile; and often I have thought since, how easy it is to be mistaken.

4 HIGH HEELS & KISSES

She called him in from the garden to lend a hand. It was her domain.
Though he came in twice a day for coffee and tea, he did so, implicitly,
not by right, but by invitation. He took his sandwiches out in the shed.
He took his boots off at the back door.

She had kissed him once at Christmas, beneath mistletoe that she
clasped, taking him by surprise, full on the lips, so fast he had not the
time to kiss her back but stood open mouthed as she stepped away.

This day she was re-laying an ancient runner in one of the
corridors; a carpet of eastern origin, faded but still beautiful. There was
an underlay of grey felt, splashed with red.

If you lift it from this end, she said, then lay it back down again, I'll
try to get the underlay straight.

He picked up the two corners, raising the carpet higher as he backed away from her until it hung a curtain between them. She went down on her haunches, pulling the underlay into place, and the light from the open door into the small parlour caught the sheen of her tights.

That's it, she said, tugging the thick fabric, now come forward.

He shuffled towards her, pushing the carpet into place with his toes, trying to keep the line, lowering it as he came. She stood up and stepped back before him. Slowly he laid down the edge, first bending, and then kneeling as he followed it down, still holding the two corners, which he laid at her feet.

Pivoting on the spike of her heel, she moved her left foot and gently placed it on the knuckles of his right hand. Neither of them spoke. He did not try to pull away, nor did she bear down upon him with her weight. He twisted his head to look up at her. She did not bend her head but he could see her eyes looking down on him.

He lowered his head and gently, in the scoop of her shoe, kissed her foot, feeling the mesh of her tights rough against his lips.

Hello? Hello? A voice called from the direction of the front door. She withdrew her foot and stepped across him.

.

5 PERHAPS TOMORROW

The tourist comes down to the pier to watch the mid-day boat come in each day. On the third day he pulls up a chair next to the old man who sits nursing his usual glass of local beer at the harbour-side bar. They have exchanged glances before, but not yet spoken.

There's nothing to see when the boat comes in, nothing exciting that is. It swings wide to the landing place, nosing bow first to the concrete slipway, its hull drawn alongside the pier. Seamen throw ropes to men on the pier who make them fast to steel bollards. The bows swing upwards like a knight's visor, and the vehicle ramps are lowered. There is the clatter of metal against concrete, and the sound of engines revving as the cars and lorries turn on their ignitions. The old man is watching intently, his fingers curled tightly around the base of his glass. The tourist wonders what it is that has so caught his attention.

Cars roll off and begin to stream away. Foot passengers, who disembark via a metal staircase wheeled up to the opening in an upper deck, spread slowly across the pier. Some go to the souvenir shop, some to the ferry office, some to the small café, some to the harbour-side bar. A few, ignoring all that, walk straight on to the bus stop, and others plod the long straight road into the hinterland of the island.

The farmer arrives in his pick-up truck just before the boat docks. He can see the vessel approaching from his fields high up on the hillside, and has got used to judging it just right.

The old man turns toward the sound of the pick-up, which because of a patched exhaust pipe is distinctive. He watches as the farmer parks, kills the engine and gets out. The farmer does not approach the pier, but stands beside his vehicle, watching the passengers disembark. Because the sun is bright he raises one clean hand to his forehead to shade his eyes. He glances briefly over towards the bar.

The old man turns away. He too scans the disembarking passengers, but he has no need to shield his eyes for there is a canvas awning over the outside tables.

What's he waiting for? The tourist asks. He has noticed the old man, and the farmer, and the fact that the old man watches the farmer with deliberate curiosity. They are of similar ages. Perhaps, the tourist thinks, they were at school together, though neither acknowledges that the other has seen him.

The old man, hearing the question does not turn to answer, but keeps his eyes fixed on the disembarking passengers. He slowly lifts his drink and sips at it before returning the glass to the table. The air is dry and crisp and hot and carries no tang of the salt water that lies so close to where they are sitting. There is not the slightest breeze. Gulls hang in the sky, riding the thermals above the boat's red funnels.

He's hoping his wife will come back to him, the old man says, still staring straight ahead.

His wife? The tourist exclaims. Has she been gone long?

Two years, the old man says, thereabouts; a little over. She left in May.

But what makes him think she'll come back this week?

He doesn't think she will, the old man says. He hopes.

The tourist frowns.

You mean?

He comes here every day, the old man says; at least, every day that the ferry comes in. The old man twists in his chair and looks back toward the hillside, as if the bar were not behind him. He can see it a long way off, he says.

But…. The tourist does not known what he wants to say, but the old man anticipates his question.

He has no way of knowing, the old man says.

But that's crazy, the tourist says.

The old man turns to look at him. His eyes look tired, as if he has watched for too long.

Do you think so?

The foot passengers have all disembarked.

The vehicles, twenty or so cars, two coaches and an articulated lorry, preceded by two motorcyclists in black leathers, have all cleared the ramp and slipway and have driven away. Crew members in garish yellow jackets have already beckoned forward the vehicles for the return journey, a couple with push bikes leading the way. There foot passengers have already ascended and the stairway is being manhandled back into its place on the pier, a long thin oblong, de-marked by faded white lines painted on the pale surface.

What if she never shows up? The tourist asks

The old man winces, as if the bright sun has suddenly shone into his eyes. He takes a longer pull at his beer, almost emptying the glass.

What can he do? The old man asks. If she does arrive, he must be there, or the chance will be lost.

What chance?

The chance to win her back.

Wouldn't she phone first?

The old man glances at him, but says nothing.

I mean, wouldn't she want him to know, if she had decided?

The old man grimaces, as if a weak joke has been attempted.

Ah! Marriane, the old man says. That would not suit her game.

The tourist puffs out his cheeks.

Some game!

The game of life, the old man says, is played out to the bitter end. He turns his head again, leaning to see beyond the tourist to where the farmer has got back into his vehicle and is reversing to turn. The old man watches until the pick-up with its noisy exhaust has driven away.

Not today then, the tourist says.

Not today, the old man echoes. He picks up the glass and drains his beer. He seems suddenly relaxed, and gazes around him as if noticing for the first time that the day is bright and warm. The mid-summer sun is dazzling off the concrete. The sea is calm and deep blue, dazzling to silver where it laps the concrete piles of the pier.

Another? The tourist asks, reaching for his wallet.

The old man raises a splayed hand in refusal, and smiling shakes his head. He pushes himself to his feet and leaves, saying, perhaps tomorrow.

6 PERHAPS TODAY

The man notices the woman when he arrives, too early, at the quayside.

He buys coffee, and takes the cardboard cup to an adjoining bench, but

not so close as to intrude. There is a stillness about the woman that

cloaks her, and arouses his curiosity. She stares beyond the harbour

with an intensity that might pull the far shore to her, or push it away.

The man sips his coffee, and is imagining a conversation, when he

senses a change in the woman, though she has not straightened her

back, or taken a quick inward breath. He follows her gaze until he finds

a mark on the horizon, and, as if they are together, they watch the dark

smudge grow until it becomes the incoming ferry. Around them, activity

mounts. A line forms of cars, coaches, lorries, and two leather clad motorcyclists who straddle their bikes at the start of the queue, like outriders.

The man begins to doubt that the woman intends to board, and he sprints to join the last straggle of foot passengers. When she finally makes her move the woman is hurried up the steps by a member of the crew. The man is aware of her then at his back, as surely as if she rested her open hand on his shoulder. They move along to the end of the deck.

The ferry pulls away from the quay. The man puts sunglasses on, and rests his arms on the white painted rail. The woman sits sideways on the slatted seat and, if he turns his head slightly, he can see her profile. In this arrangement, he feels able at last to speak to her.

'Amazing weather. Are you on holiday?' He glances at the small holdall by the woman's feet. 'Or coming back?' he inclines his head in the direction the boat is taking. 'Going home?'

'Going back,' she says. 'Perhaps.'

He decides not to be deterred by her ambiguity. 'I'm told it's a beautiful place this time of year,' he says and is ridiculously pleased by her small smile, even though he knows it is not for him.

The woman is remembering another bright summer's day, and another man, a man who thought too much, and who saw her as his problem, a dilemma that he would resolve in time. She thinks now that she might have waited for him to solve her with his words, and his sense of fair play, and his sibling loyalty, then remembers how she tired of the game. And so it was his brother who followed her to the shore that day, he in his stiff, work boots, and her on soft, pale tiptoes, strands of seaweed laced between her fingers. Always sure footed, she slipped that day, and was pulled to him, and he laughed to hear her name the grey seals for their differences. He said they all appeared alike to him and she overlooked that, because he told her he knew each of his cows by their shadows alone.

The boat moves now in a wide arc, as if to surprise the approaching harbour by aiming for a point somewhere to the right. The man frowns, but the woman knows the change in direction is to counteract the strong undercurrent, and she enjoys the swell of energy surging beneath.

'Bit bleak in winter, I imagine. A tight knit community I expect.' The man cannot help but talk to her. 'You are local?'

'No, not local.' She thinks she can already see the small town sitting around the harbour, waiting to judge her. Two brothers were born in the farmhouse, on the hill above the town, within sight of the shore. And the one must write about how the ocean could lie soft as stroked satin, or roar in to relieve the shores from boredom. About the whiskered seals, who elbowed their tight, dappled bodies onto rocks to take the sun. And the other was all about tractors, livestock, and harvesting, and the thought strikes her, as if for the first time, that he was earth and she was water, and that became their problem.

And the one who made her his problem saw that words were not enough and he leaves before he can imagine his brother returning from the heat of the fields and her eyes closing as she licks the salt from his skin, and pushes her fingers across his back.

The woman closes her eyes now, fidgets on the seat, stands and puts both hands on the outer rail, watches the water churn and froth from under the boat. When she opens her eyes she sees that the man has taken off his sunglasses to watch her.

Like an image coming into focus, the buildings beyond the pier become defined. Houses emerge whose shapes are familiar to her, except that their walls are now splashed in seaside colours, as if they all wear their holiday clothes. A line of cars and trucks wait for the incoming ferry, and the heavy smell of diesel drifts to her as the boat lines up with the concrete slipway. She sees that the old boathouse has been transformed into a harbour-side bar with a striped canvas awning. Tables are arranged in its narrow shade and two men sit at one of them, the pale ovals of their faces turned towards the ferry.

Close enough now, she sees one of the men at the table twist in his seat, and there is something so recognisable, so known to her, about the tilt of his head and the angle of his body that she has to look away, up the hill, but the farmhouse waits there, so she finds the lane that meanders back between hedges. The lane unravels into the village, disappears behind buildings, and emerges ahead of a pick-up truck that stops, two wheels on the grass, two on the tarmac.

A man climbs down from the truck, as if he has done this a

thousand times. As the ferry's ramp hits the concrete slipway he slams the door of the pick-up, and lifts his hand to his brow in one quick, familiar movement. From beneath his curved fingers he stares at the boat, and the air is suddenly too dry, too hot for her to breathe. Her grip tightens on the rail until a patch of rust flakes and is sharp under her palm.

She waves away the man's expression of concern, and his offer of bottled water. Reluctantly, he walks to where the remaining foot passengers are now moving down the metal staircase. He looks back, thinking that the woman was the last to board, and will be the last to leave. But she is seated now, straight backed, and her face turned so that she doesn't see him, or the harbour, or the farmhouse on the hill.

7 BOOKMARKED

Ruth spent Christmas day alone, but she has no problems with this. It has been a quiet but pleasant day and she is looking forward to the pleasure of a visit from her son, Mark, on Boxing Day. Ruth knows how busy he has been over the last few weeks and she is all set to spoil him a little with his favourite food.

Ruth props herself up against the pillows, steadies her reading glasses, and opens a paperback book. The novel is one of her Christmas gifts, sent by Mark. She reads until sleep approaches then continues to the end of the current page, as is her habit. She turns to the next page and is about to rest a bookmark there when she notices a dark hair stretched across the page. Ruth frowns. She considers the hair. She tilts the book a little and then, as if it were a birthday candle, she blows it from the book and leans over the side of the bed to see it land in front of the bedside table. She watches it for a moment, as if the small scene might rewind and so return the hair to the page.

Ruth sighs. Fully awake now, she contemplates the book anew. She imagines Mark browsing the shelves of his local bookstore. He would be attracted to this title, or that author or, as she herself often was, be drawn to the style of the lettering on the spine or to an appealing cover design. More likely, Mark knew exactly which book he was going to buy for her, she thinks, and smiles to herself; they know each other's tastes so well.

From when he was a small child, teachers would comment on his gentle, quiet nature. They didn't understand him as she did. Mark was a thoughtful boy and preferred to observe life, rather than racket about, as other boys did. Ruth glanced towards the window and, though the curtains were closed, she could visualise the garden at the rear of the house and the broad branch of the old tree that Mark used to climb towards as soon as he returned home from school. Even as a teenager, he would sit up there for hours. There were times when Ruth had to walk out to the tree and call his name to bring him in for meals.

Ruth took another look at the hair where it lay, dark against the carpet. Not one of Mark's fair hairs, certainly. And not one of her own grey hairs. A stranger's hair then. Ruth is unsure of this thought but she follows it. Someone in the store took down the book, her book. They opened it at this page or that, but it didn't suit and so they returned it to the shelf. It was a woman, a young woman, Ruth decides, whose dark hair fell loosely over her slim shoulders. And a length of her hair caught, as she closed the book. She most likely frowned, thinks Ruth, and perhaps pulled her head back sharply. No, this was a pleasant natured girl, Ruth decides, who smiled and gently freed her hair.

Perhaps Mark was there too, waiting patiently for an opportunity to browse the same shelves when the girl moved away. Ruth leans back and smiles again. Mark would see what had happened and the two of them would share a look of complicity, as you do sometimes with a stranger. Then the look would linger, she decides, because Mark could be so charming, with his shy smile and blue eyes; the blue eyes that her grandchildren might inherit if only Mark were a little less shy.

The events that follow the meeting of Mark, and the dark haired girl, progress quickly now. Ruth recalls Mark saying he had started his Christmas shopping early this year. Plenty of time then for the relationship to progress, from Mark's tentative suggestion of a coffee in the bookstore cafe, to proper dates; the cinema, dinner and the discovery of the interests that they shared. For Claire, as Ruth temporarily names her, is also a gentle, book-loving soul whose shyness has, until now, prevented her from meeting a future husband. Like Mark, she too is interested in interior design and also has an apartment that she has skilfully decorated and furnished. With both apartments sold, Mark and Claire would have the funds to find a small family property with two, or even three, bedrooms.

And so another small boy, Daniel, would have silky fair hair that Ruth would comb and tidy, after he too had climbed the old tree in the garden. As she hugs this thought to herself, almost at once, a little girl,

Rosie, takes shape. The girl has Claire's dark hair, tidied into two glossy braids, and she has been helping Ruth to ice the little cakes they have made together. Rosie sees her brother through the kitchen window. She passes on details to Ruth of how he has twigs in his hair, and they share comments about the silliness of brothers and of small boys in general. Oh, thinks Ruth, such delights.

The thought now occurs to her that Claire might even have wrapped the book and she wishes she had taken more notice of the wrapping paper to see if it differed in any way from the tasteful paper and ribbon that Mark always chose. The gift tag had Mark's name alone on it, but he would not want to spoil his news, thinks Ruth, by including Claire's name. Mark and Claire wrapping Christmas gifts together. Soul mates, thinks Ruth, and next Christmas there will be teddies to wrap.

She retrieves the hair and replaces it in the book, more securely than before. It lies now along the centre groove, as if uniting the two pages on either side. She discards the leather bookmark and settles herself for sleep.

The following morning, she is in the hall when she hears Mark's car pull into the drive. Through the frosted glass of the inner door, she is not surprised to see two people enter the porch or to observe that the two figures merge into a single blurred shape. Ruth pulls open the door.

The man, whose arm is around her son's waist, seems to fill the porch with his bulk and Ruth must step backwards to find a place from where she can take in all of it. She sees the heart tattooed on the back of the man's hand and the four letters of her son's name, black across crimson. She sees the oil stained t-shirt, the gold that pierces both eyebrows, and she sees the dark hair, tied back in a greasy ponytail.

8 IF THE OCEANS RISE

The interior of the car was too hot, the sun on the windscreen too bright. Every set of traffic lights flicked to red as she approached. Every pedestrian crossing was a bridge, over a chasm, across which people crawled. When she swung the car up the slope to reverse into her parking space, the engine stalled. She let the car roll back and it stopped short; just.

A man leant against the back door of the pub. He watched her with narrowed eyes, a cigarette pinched between his fingers. She turned the ignition key with a soft curse for yet another failure, and reversed the car over the last metre of loose gravel that crunched and rolled beneath the tyres. Dragging bags across from the passenger seat, she shifted them around awkwardly as she got out of the car and closed the door with her hip.

Though the sound was small, it caught her attention. A bird, unkempt, ragged, and with a half feathered scrawny neck hopped out from between the rear wheels of the car. It hunched squawking at the base of the wall. She saw how easily she could have driven over it, been unaware of snapped bones and twisted feathers. As she bent over the bird it hopped clumsily and stretched inadequate wings. She leaned in closer. The bird bobbed up and down as if hoping that an ability to fly had developed during the time it had been grounded.

'Young Jackdaw is it?'

He startled her. The man from the pub was at her shoulder.

'I think so.' She looked up into an empty sky. 'I expect the parent birds will come back for it.'

'What can they do?'

'They could feed it.'

'It's not going to survive long here though, is it?' He dropped easily into a crouch and the bird shuffled backwards in alarm.

She hesitated, rearranged the bags in her arms, glanced at her watch, sighed. Now she must give some thought to a bird, on top of everything else.

'You going to work then?' He stood up, and gave a sideways nod to the back door of the library, and she nodded in return. 'I've seen you before.' With a twist of one heel he crushed the cigarette end he had dropped. 'Going in there, I mean.'

She glanced at him then. There was a watchfulness about him, and an underlying quiet persistence that unnerved her. He could, she felt, stay his hand in any situation until exactly the right moment.

'You must like books then.'

'Don't you enjoy reading?'

He grinned. 'What do you think?'

The bird cocked its head at them, as if their conversation had become so interesting that its own vulnerable position was momentarily forgotten.

'Never read a book in my life.' He pushed his hands into the pockets of his jeans and rocked on his heels a little. The thought struck her that there was a look of the rodeo about him. It was more than the checked shirt, and the weathered brown of his skin. She saw him driving cattle, throwing a circle of rope around the neck of an unbroken pony, biding his time until the animal stilled and allowed him to rest one hand on its trembling flanks. 'Never bothered much with school either.' He threw this in as a statement of fact without defiance or apology.

She thought of her own conviction that learning was everything, and books the portal to new worlds of knowledge. Words shaped her life. Words were her pleasure, her escape, and that someone should be so careless of them was shocking to her.

'You don't read?'

'Not unless I have to.'

'What, not even newspapers?'

'Especially not newspapers.'

'But how do you learn anything new?'

'Is there so much that's new?'

'Of course there is. You can't live in some kind of bubble. The world around us is constantly developing and progressing. It's changing all the time. '

'People don't change though.'

'People change most of all.' Her voice was bitter. He raised one eyebrow.

She cleared her throat. 'There are things you need to be aware of, surely?' She cast around for an example. 'What about global warming?'

'I heard about that. Not going to happen.'

She was incredulous. 'How can you say that? There's evidence already. Ice caps melting, massive fluctuations in weather...'

'Weather has always been changeable. Ask any farmer.'

'Well that's great. Thanks for the reassurance. Now that I know for sure that flooding of biblical proportions isn't heading our way, I can relax.'

'Seems to me that you need to relax anyway.' He smiled at her. 'Tell you what, if I'm wrong, and the oceans rise, then I will build a boat, and sail to where you are.'

Above them an aircraft wrote its passing in a lazy trail of white vapour.

With a harsh squawk, the bird ripped a hole in their word filled silence.

'Maybe the best thing would be to wring its neck,' he said, illustrating his words with a quick twisting movement of both hands. '

She looked at him in horror. 'No! It deserves a chance. It might fly.'

'Lot of flapping, but no flying as far as I can see. Might be kinder to finish it now than leave it here until it knows it's not going anywhere.'

There were boxes in the office. She could catch the bird, take it somewhere, the RSPCA maybe? But then it would be in the office all day, scratching over the cardboard, a frantic rustling in captivity. He watched her.

'Lot of trouble to go to for a bird I'd say, and it would probably die anyway if it's put in a box. Some creatures give up the will to live if they're trapped.'

She pushed her arms through the handles of bags, freed a bunch of keys with difficulty, and unlocked the door. In the cool inner passage the alarm buzzed and as she reached up to switch it off the base of one carrier bag gave way, spilling its contents around her feet. A hardback book dropped heavily on corners that buckled and bent. Paperbacks fluttered open before landing face down.

When she stepped back outside he was waiting still, and so was the bird.

'Do it now,' she said.

9 SLEEPING

The journey took longer than expected. The delays were longer than advised. Colin and Jane pushed through a noisy crowd of football supporters, up concrete steps to the footbridge, and from there out into a wet night that smelled of diesel fumes and damp coats. A member of staff held an important clipboard and pointed to a line of coaches. He told them where to stand, and how sorry he was for any inconvenience.

They were beyond further talk of the day spent in meetings, and were too weary to protest about the wait for a replacement bus. In silence they stood until shepherded aboard the coach that was to take them to the destination printed on their rail tickets so long ago.

On the coach Colin stood to one side to allow Jane to slide across to the seat by the window. Both knew how little there would be to see at night on the motorway, but the concession was always offered, and always accepted. Jane took off her raincoat and rolled it lengthways so that the lining shone outwards. Colin carefully folded it in half and placed it on the overhead rack. She straightened her jacket to avoid creasing, and smoothed the matching trousers. Half heartedly they brought out folders from briefcases, and papers from folders, as the coach filled around them with assorted passengers.

The interior lights dimmed as the coach groaned into dull streets with nothing to offer but the brick ghosts of an industrial past. After narrow terraced rows, bay windowed suburbs evolved, lining a ring road until finally the motorway was announced on large signs.

Jane gave up on any further work. She put away the papers and the briefcase, placed her hands tidily, one over the other on her lap and closed her eyes. Colin leaned his head against the seat back that was never the right height for comfort. Across the aisle from him a young woman was curled against the side of the seat, her face tilted towards him. She had one hand cushioned beneath her chin, and draped across her, like an autumn quilt, was a russet coloured, woollen coat.

As Colin watched her, the woman softened and sank into sleep. She was so close to him that, without fully stretching his arm, he could have brushed her lips with his fingertips. He saw her thighs relax, soften, and her knees part beneath the coat as her body became drowsy. Her eyelashes drooped, and rested long upon her cheek, and the fine strands of hair loose over her face, lifted and fell with the in and the out of her breath.

He sensed his wife shifting beside him. When he looked, though her back was still straight, Jane had allowed her chin to lower onto her chest. A small bulge of flesh had been pushed around the sharp point of her chin. She slept, he thought, exactly as she carried herself when awake; in an upright, dignified manner. Colin thought of all the journeys they had made together. All the business trips, the delayed trains and replacement buses, all the weary into the night travelling and he realised, like a slap in the face, that Jane had never rested her head against his shoulder in sleep. She had never curled against him for comfort. Jane slept in a straight line in their bed, and by morning had barely creased the sheets.

The woman moved now, as if to draw him back to her. Her mouth had curved into a small smile and he wondered if she was dreaming, but she frowned then in her sleep and gave a little murmur, as if he had intruded. She slept as if no one could see her. She was warm, yielding femininity and he felt her challenge the cold greyness of him. Everything; his suit, tie, raincoat, umbrella, all his neutral, neutered, greyscale existence was somehow lacking, and had always fallen short of a life filled with colour. This woman, he thought, would sleep with abandon. She would be restless, sleep diagonally, rumple the sheets, turn the pillows around. In the morning, he thought, you would know she had been there.

As the coach neared the railway station where they were to

disembark in some pretence of having completed the whole journey by train, he chivvied his wife into her coat, stood in the aisle, said he wanted to get ahead of the crush. And all the while he sensed the woman waking at his back; heard her yawns and soft sighs, the rustle as she pulled on her coat. He made sure they left her behind as they hurried to the car park. There would be someone waiting for her, of course.

Driving past the station they were held in a queue of home going commuters. As Jane sighed and stared wearily beyond the steering wheel, Colin saw the woman waiting at the station entrance. He wanted to look away, but she smiled and waved in his direction. He almost raised his own hand when he saw that a man had crossed the road between the standing traffic and had emerged from behind their car to walk towards the woman.

Colin watched as the man reached her, hugged her to him, pushed his hands into her hair and covered her face with small kisses that made her laugh. She reached up and tousled his thinning grey hair. It began to rain and the man held out one side of his dark raincoat, a wing that she tucked herself beneath to become a splash of colour against his pin striped suit.

10 WATER WINGS

The bus lurches through traffic lights towards the stop. Maggie looks ahead to see if anyone is waiting to get on. She feels that she has set a simple, but fair, test. At this time of the morning most people are heading into the city centre, rather than back towards the suburbs, so the chances of anyone waiting there are slim. That it must be a woman in order to pass the test is, of course, an additional obstacle. Yet there she is, a young woman, who waits patiently for Maggie, and her suitcase, to leave the bus. That is the first sign.

Maggie drags the wheeled suitcase behind her. She is careful to avoid the uneven areas of pavement and she lifts the suitcase up and down kerbs when crossing the road. Her leather shoulder bag is securely slung across her body, and in her free hand she carries a plastic bag from which the end of a towel pokes out, like a Swiss roll. The suitcase has been packed for weeks, but the towel was freshly rolled that morning. From time to time she looks from one to the other, as if they were decisions to be made.

Ahead of her, she sees a dark haired man striding vigorously, the briefcase he carries in one hand swinging back and forth at the same brisk pace. Her stomach contracts and she almost calls out to him, but the man turns to cross the road and Maggie sees that he is a stranger. Still, she watches him until he reaches the far kerb, even though she understands that his hair is darker, that he is younger, and that the briefcase he carries is black and not tan.

Maggie swims at the municipal pool every Wednesday. This leaves her enough time to walk to her job in the city centre accountant's office. As she approaches the entrance she sees that Sue is behind the reception desk. Maggie takes a breath - this is the second sign.

Sue smiles a good morning at Maggie and accepts temporary responsibility of the suitcase. She asks her if she is going anywhere nice but the telephone rings before Maggie need answer and she is able to slip away, down the stairs to the changing rooms.

The communal changing area is empty but still Maggie uses a cubicle to undress and pull on her swimsuit. She stretches the fabric, pulls and arranges until satisfied that there is maximum coverage.

At the poolside she backs down the dimpled rungs of the steel ladder and sinks into the water, shivering past the initial, stomach gripping chill. She checks that the lane is free and launches herself into a smooth breaststroke. And then all there is the methodical upward push of her thin shoulders through the water. Maggie feels stronger when swimming and

lately she has glimpsed the possibility of such forward momentum being transferred to her life on dry land.

She joins other regular swimmers as they move in an orderly manner up and down the pool with even strokes. Maggie has set herself a target of an additional 5 lengths over her usual 20. She settles into a smooth pace and then increases speed gradually. As she turns on each length, she twists to look up at the large clock. On the twentieth length, she knows that her goal is within reach. That will be the final sign.

She is three quarters of the way through her 22nd length when, seemingly out of nowhere, a woman veers into her lane a little ahead of her, cutting across her path abruptly. The woman flips onto her back and, with windmill arms, powers away from Maggie, her large, water-wing breasts flowing at one with the water. In their natural element, they undulate from side to side. They create their own wash. Beyond the woman's flailing limbs all is gaping mouth and flared nostrils.

Satisfied that her pace was uninterrupted, despite the woman's interference, and that she is still on track for the extra 5 lengths, Maggie dips deep underwater, with renewed confidence and strength. As she thrusts her body upwards, the woman approaches the far end of the pool where she does a backwards somersault. In a turmoil of water her feet engage with the side. She pushes violently to propel herself forwards again and, against all pool etiquette, the woman emerges directly in front of Maggie once again.

She is the cross channel ferry to Maggie's dinghy. Maggie coughs, splutters, inhales water and flails to the side. The woman continues without pause. Eyes streaming and throat constricting, she sees the suitcase emptied, the new dress hanging again in her wardrobe, silk and lace returned to the chest of drawers. And she tastes the bitterness of it as plainly as she tastes the salt on her face.

Maggie hauls herself onto the ladder. A heaviness of water sluices down her body as if it were trying to drag her back into the pool. She snatches for her towel but it falls from the slatted wooden bench. Aware of the intimate angle her skinny rear end would present to those at water level, Maggie does not bend to retrieve it. She makes a grab for the towel from a self-conscious, sideways crouch. She swaddles her body with it and glances behind her. No one is looking.

In the changing area she manages the locker key and the coin mechanism without losing her grip on the towel. With one hand she pulls shampoo and shower gel from under her

neatly folded clothes. The woman who waterlogged Maggie appears beside her. She hums loudly as she clangs open the adjoining locker. Maggie leaves as the woman drags out a crumpled towel and begins rummaging amongst the clothes piled inside.

In the shower area Maggie hangs up her towel and stands under the end shower, the one tucked close to the tiled wall, as she always does. The showers are hot but Maggie shivers as she massages shampoo into her hair. She tilts her head back to rinse.

'I know it's a cheek but I forgot my shower stuff today and I wondered if I could have a couple of squirts of yours?'

Maggie turns, a froth of soap suds pale on her black swimsuit. The woman is naked. Beyond her, Maggie sees a large striped swimsuit hanging on a hook next to a bright pink towel. Unable to meet the woman's eyes, Maggie offers her agreement in the direction of the generous breasts that wobble, alert and cheerful, and too close to her.

'Best bit, don't you think?' the woman says, stooping to pick up Maggie's shampoo. 'A lovely hot shower.'

Maggie wraps her arms around her ribs and lets the water rinse over her.

The woman continues to make conversation, making it difficult for Maggie to turn away. She is astonished at the utter lack of self awareness as the woman raises her arms to knead shampoo into her scalp. Her bosom also makes a half hearted attempt to rise. The woman bends again to exchange shampoo for shower gel and then Maggie hears, as if it were amplified, the slap and squeeze of many curves and crevices as they are thoroughly lathered.

Later, Maggie is elbowing the sides of the narrow cubicle and hopping from one foot to the other whilst struggling into clothes that stick to her damp skin, when she hears the woman humming, in the open changing area. And she knows that the woman will be towelling her body vigorously and scrupulously.

When Maggie emerges, fully dressed, the woman is hoisting up a generous undergarment. She squats broadly to adjust the elasticated legs to her satisfaction and comfort.

'I beat my personal best today,' she says to Maggie with a grin. 'And beat it by five lengths. Five lengths!' She gives herself a nod of congratulation and leans forward to manoeuvre her breasts into a stately bra. A showgirl wriggle of her shoulders gathers all in and the creamy surface of her breasts settles with a final quiver.

'Has to be some sort of sign don't you think?' She nods again, but this time directs it at Maggie.

Maggie stares at her.

'Maybe it's a sign that I'm getting better at this swimming lark at last.'

Maggie walks slowly towards the stairwell and takes the last set of stairs two steps at a time.

In Reception, Sue smiles at Maggie and pushes the suitcase out to her.

'You have a lovely time now.'

Outside, Maggie walks quickly and decisively. The suitcase rattles along behind her as if trying to keep up with this new and impetuous mistress. Hurrying into the railway station, she takes out the ticket that he has sent her, every month, since she last saw him. She holds the edges of it carefully, as if it were a photograph. Stopping to buy coffee from the kiosk she takes the ribbed cardboard cup onto the train with her, managing coffee and suitcase with ease, confidently, as if it were not her first time.

Maggie looks through the window as the train moves off, and the platform begins to slide past. Through the blurred reflection of her own smile, she sees a woman stop, and consider the rolled up towel that drips from a station bench.

ABOUT THE AUTHORS

Brindley Hallam Dennis writes short stories, many of which have been published and performed. He has won numerous prizes and awards (writing, as Mike Smith, poetry, plays and essays).
He blogs at www.Bhdandme.wordpress.com/
and is on Vimeo at BHDandMe
His Twitter handle is @BHDandMe
He runs Facets of *Fic*tion an ongoing writers' workshop

Marilyn Messenger writes short stories from the English side of the Solway Firth. Her stories have been published in various magazines, read at book festivals, and performed at Liars league, New York.
Her Twitter handle is @marilynmessengr

Made in the USA
Charleston, SC
25 March 2015